THE STOAT–WEASEL



Gordon Vells works as a translator and editor from his home, close to the point where the counties of Dorset, Somerset and Wiltshire meet.

*The Stoat–Weasel Interface* is his third full-length poetry collection, completing a trilogy along with *Plundered by Lobsters* and *Wasp Disentanglement for Beginners*.

Gordon Vells is a pen-name.

More poetry by Gordon Vells in Xenon Lobster Books:

*Plundered by Lobsters*

*On Wings*

*Wasp Disentanglement for Beginners*

# *The* Stoat–Weasel Interface

*Poems of light, life and mustelids*

Gordon Vells

Xenon Lobster Books

First published in 2025 by Xenon Lobster Books



ISBN 978-1-326-27883-0

Typeset in Constantia

Printed by Lulu.com

Xenon Lobster Books
Staddle Stones, Wyke Road, Gillingham,
Dorset SP8 4NG, England

www.xenonlobster.co.uk
@xenonlobster

*For my family.*

# Contents

# Stoats, weasels and ermines

genus *Mustela*, subgenus *Mustela*

The Greek term for weasel, *νυφίτσα*, means "little bride".
It's probably inadvisable to refer to weasels
as "bridelets", though.

## The Stoat–Weasel Interface

Stoats and weasels look quite similar,
but there are some important differences.
The following may help you
to distinguish between the species.

Firstly, stoats are slightly larger
and have a long tail with a black tip;
weasels' tails are stubbier, without the black end.

Stoats move with a bounding gait,
their back arched, whereas
weasels move quickly, staying flat to the ground.

Stoats smell of freshly mown grass,
weasels of newsprint.

Both stoats and weasels have a diet of small rodents,
rabbits, birds, eggs and worms.
Stoats will also eat fruit
(tinned lychees are a particular favourite).
Weasels will chew paper, but not for food:
they like to make replica wasp nests to relax.

Stoats make a high-pitched hiss or shriek when alarmed;
weasels feign death and use meditation techniques
until they regain composure.

Stoats dream in colour;
weasels dream in sound.

# THE STOAT–WEASEL INTERFACE

Stoats like revolutionary Russian poets,
but weasels prefer Hispanophone writers:
Lorca, Neruda, Borges.

Stoats look good in a trilby;
weasels, due to their colouring,
can carry off a panama.

Stoats are naturally talented at interior design
and soft furnishings.
By contrast, weasels often excel at creative metalwork.

When photographed, stoats will pose for the camera
then look with fascination at the picture.
Weasels, however, tend to
vibrate at a frequency that makes them invisible to digital
    cameras;
we recommend taking Polaroids instead.

When they meet,
stoats and weasels generally keep a respectful distance from
    each other:
weasels are mindful of stoats' greater size and strength;
stoats acknowledge weasels' cunning
and superiority at solving cryptic crosswords.

Both species, however, defer to badgers,
the senior mustelids.
And they all distrust mink.

## Grey and Yellow

The bloke at 21's got a Morris Minor:
Dead Mouse Grey, shiny hubcaps.

Schoolday mornings, he backs it out the garage
with all the care of a new dad with a pram;

and while he's closing the up-and-over door
his children honk the horn, laugh, squeal.

When driving it he wears a fluorescent vest –
just in case, you know. Just in case.

## Parabola

Blackbird flutters up;
injured, impaired,
inadequate flight
describes parabolic arc

back to the hands of
the woman aching
to provide care;
it submits to her gentle grasp.

She juggles eager whippet
and becalmed patient.

The immediate drama past,
we pass,
exchange nods,
awkward, no-teeth smiles;

we both know it was her dog's teeth
that she rescued the bird from
and now she is burdened
with two souls' welfare.

## The Ermine's Point of View

They say white-on-white's a strong look,
but I don't do this for fashion
or (Mighty Badger!) cricket.

*You* try blending in in the woods
when you're in your winter finery
and the snow's not come.

They say it's an honour
to be worn by a monarch,
but they are not an ermine.

They say that an ermine would rather
surrender to hunters than soil its pure white fur,
but they are not an ermine.

Think I'm cute, do you?
Go on then. Pick me up.
These teeth can go clean to the bone.

## Brushes

These paintbrushes read “Sable/synthetic blend”.
Compromise.
And not in fact sable hair, but Siberian weasel.
Bent truth?
*Vozmozhno* – perhaps.

But how is the hair harvested from their tails?
A gentle stroking process as they purr?
Or is there trapping?
Panic? Termination?
*Vozmozhno* – perhaps.

Might they be caught and destroyed anyway
by Russian farmers
to stop the weasels killing their chickens?
Aren’t they just pests?
*Vozmozhno* – perhaps.

Are ethics complicated?
*Vozmozhno* – perhaps.

## The Man in the Moon Sends a Voice Note

I know we haven't been in contact for a while
you sent some chaps with candles
a few years ago was it
I left out cookies but they didn't seem to notice

I hope all is well with you
from over here it's hard to tell
but your garden it still looks beautiful
me I try to keep the craters tidy and welcoming

## Remedies Derived from the Weasel

Pliny the Elder, in his *Natural History,**
drily asserts that the flesh of the weasel,
"preserved in salt, is given, in doses
of one denarius, in three cyathi of drink
to persons who have been stung by serpents".
We deride such delusion, yet gulp down
modern remedies to the bite of the snake:
"Buying this thing will improve your life."

---

* Pliny the Elder, *Naturalis Historia*, Book 29, chapter 16 (translated by John Bostock and H.T. Riley)

## Afternoon on the Ward

Just another afternoon on the ward:
the fitful awareness,
the care assistants,
the family and friends around the beds,
the screams that make the air bleed.

*Murderers* is what she shouts, mostly –
*Murder on this ward* –
punctuated by howls
that exceed workplace safe decibel limits.
*Murder in Wiltshire.*

The airy four-bed bay has panoramic glass,
and the low, winter sun warms the blankets,
the lidded jug of water,
the unread book,
the blue plastic chairs.

*Dirt-ridden mausoleum,* comes the shout from the corridor.
*Demolition!* a legion screams.

*You're all from the cesspit,*
*and that's where you belong with your filthy germs.*

*You devil! Get out the way, you devil –*
*and filthy with it.*

*Go down into hell.*
*I hope you go blood red with all your lies.*

*You're going to be buried alive.*
*Death to all of you. Death!*

*You damned hypocrite, parading your wares.*
*You'll be there for holy communion, you wait and see.*

*Come on! Come on! Kill them all on this ward.*
*Kill them all tonight! Murder. Murder! Get them!*

*If you get out of this ward . . . they eat your flesh.*
*Devils, devils, devils.*

*You're killers, killers of the good and the simple-minded.*
*They'll kill you and flay you to bits, just you wait.*

*Wiltshire murders! Wiltshire murders!*
*The crematorium!*

*Murderers,* she yells, as a nurse passes her.
"Good afternoon, Elsie," replies the nurse,
with all the patience and control
of one who has seen death and madness
and has come to expect it.

"It's like being in an Alan Ayckbourn play, isn't it?"
remarks the chap in the bed opposite,
chuckles, adjusts his sitting position,
winces from his broken leg.
Offstage, another harpy screech is released.

And from this bed by the window
there are expansive views

of the fields and the hills
and the vast car park
and the fresh-air asylum with its eight billion inmates.

## Time's Meadow

in time's meadow
wildflowers and measures grow side by side
the clover · the æon · the woundwort · the second
invisible purple in acres of year-grass
a habitat both bio- and chronodiverse
life-rich · time-rich

in this grassland
spiders wrap flies in silver-spun time-silk
inescapable · twisting · unidirectional
gatekeeper butterflies seek temporal nectar
eternally bittersweet · never repeating
sup the epochs

## Stoating

*(for Braz)*

It was the birdsong we noticed first –
a change in tone from brightness to agitation
that told us something was up,
an uninvited guest at the party.

The wood was pounding with springy hues –
the infinite haze of the bluebells,
the absolute snowdrift of the wild garlic,
the acid green of the spurge –

and the birds clove this rave
with their alarm-call sirens.
*I think there's a stoat around*, you said,
and then there it was, pogoing

to the beat, having the time of its life.
It had a swagger, an attitude,
not so much owning the dancefloor
as living the predator's dream,

shimmying up an oaken trunk
to check out the tasty goods, until
it was chased down by an angry squirrel
shouting and shaking its fist.

Carefree in its personal chillout room,
the stoat pronked off through the ramsons
and away down the ride
with all the insouciance of Pepé le Pew.

# Badgers

genus *Meles*

Regional names for badgers abound.
One, "bawson", means piebald (i.e. black and white);
the more widely known "brock" is of Celtic origin.
Somehow, there's something tender and familiar
about calling a badger a brock.

## About Three Dozen Badgers

Badgers are stocky, omnivorous mustelids with a distinctive striped head. Badgerline was a bus company in the south-west of England, based in Weston-super-Mare. "Badger", of uncertain etymology, is a term for an itinerant dealer in victuals. The badger game is a con in which the mark is tricked into a compromising position and then blackmailed. According to Cree oral traditions, the Cree syllabic script was invented by a man called Calling Badger (*Mistanâkôwêw*, ᒥᐢᑕᓈᑰᐍᐤ). Upshot–Knothole Badger was the sixth of eleven atmospheric nuclear weapons tests carried out in 1953 in Nevada. Little Badger Island is a small, uninhabited granite island near Tasmania. Jack Black, rat-catcher to Her Majesty Queen Victoria, used various animals to accomplish his task – typically ferrets and dogs working in partnership, but also on occasion a monkey, two raccoons and a badger called Polly. The Tupolev Tu-16 "Badger" is a jet-powered bomber built in the Soviet Union that has been in service for over seventy years. HMS *Badger* was the first Royal Navy ship commanded by Horatio Nelson. Badger is a puppet character from the children's TV show *Bodger and Badger* with a fascination for mashed potato. George Percy Badger (1815–88) was an English missionary who wrote extensively on Arabic history, the Nestorian church, Malta and the Suez Canal. Wisconsin is known as "the Badger State" due to the nineteenth-century lead miners there who lived in tunnels that they had burrowed into the hillsides. Tommy Brock is a badger from Beatrix Potter's *The Tale of Mr. Tod* who kidnaps the Flopsy Bunnies, intending to eat them. The cyclist Bernard Hinault, who won the Tour de France five times between 1978 and 1985, was nicknamed "The Badger" because of his aggressive style of riding. Breezy Badger was the code name of version 5.10 of the Linux distribution Ubuntu. Grimbart the Badger was an ally of Reynard the Fox in the medieval tales of the same name. The end of each episode of *The Harry Hill Show* was supposed to feature "The Badger Parade", starring a number of puppet badgers including Windsor Davies Badger, Tasmin Archer Badger, Gareth Southgate Badger and Michael Owen Badger; however, there would always be some sort of issue that prevented the badgers from performing. Badger Beadon is a character from the Agatha Christie novel *Why Didn't They Ask Evans?* The Battle of Badger Mouth took place in 1211 at Yehuling in China. Jon Alvie Gutierrez, also known as King Badger, is a hip-hop artist and actor from the Philippines. *Blaireau* is the French word for badger, and is also used to mean shaving brush (luxury examples being made of badger bristles) and, colloquially, "moron". George E. Badger served as the twelfth US Secretary of the Navy under presidents William Henry Harrison and John Tyler. Detective Inspector Archie LeBrock, an anthropomorphic badger, is the star of the *Grandville* series of steampunk graphic novels by Bryan Talbot. In molecular spectroscopy, Badger's rule states that the strength of a bond correlates inversely with the bond length. Lewis Carroll once described the toves of Jabberwocky as "a species of Badger [with] smooth white hair, long hind legs, and short horns like a stag," adding that they "lived chiefly on cheese". American singer-songwriter Ne-Yo competed on the second series of *The Masked Singer UK* in 2021 as the character Badger, eventually finishing second to Sausage (Joss Stone). The steamship SS *Badger* provides a ferry service across Lake Michigan, taking four hours to sail between Manitowoc, Wisconsin, and Ludington, Michigan. In *The Wind in the*

*Willows* by Kenneth Grahame, Mr. Badger is a figure embodying wisdom. Badger is a village in Shropshire, near Bridgnorth. Badger brand beer is brewed in Dorset. Badgers are still stocky, omnivorous mustelids with a distinctive striped head.

## What We See When It's Dark

When down is dark
up is where the *things* are
(the visible)
so that's where we look.

The *things* are on fire
but from where we are
they recall a living world.

The constellation in point, Cassiopeia,
pictures a seated queen, or
to the Sámi, elk antlers;
Chinese viewers saw these *things*
as a bridge of kings;
the Inuit, a lampstand;
still others, a rabbit, a spider,
a group of reindeer,
a camel, a stained hand
or a noble court.

I look up and see a W
(how literal)
while less mind-bound souls
see *things* with the eye of lifelight;

for when it is dark
and we look up at the *things*
what we see is our minds' insides.

## 6.30 p.m. in Duncliffe Wood

The A-flat thrum of woodland flies,
like a fire blowing over an open bottleneck
or distant stadia's vuvuzelas in my head;

the tension
makes my fingers twitch,
my nose hairs vibrate,
lifts me three inches clear of the ground,
only fading once I leave the wood behind.

## Roadkill

a ghastly meat bagpipe,
the ribs splayed as drones and chanter

## Flimsy

gatekeeper butterfly
trapped in cobweb
flapping forlornly
how long

I release you from the sticky silk
just one and a half wings left if that
place you on a safer leaf
walk on
can't bear to watch and see if you can even fly

later on I get caught on barbed wire
the more I flail the worse it gets
leave me here
my wings are too shredded to lift my frail body
it's not worth it

## and things

*. . . and mum mum yesterday we did science mum and we learnt about living things and non-living things and do you know what is the longest living thing and the longest non-living thing and* how do you define living and non-living now there are some non-living things that used to be living things there seems to be a lot of that at the moment and the words we use to describe things change when the things change from being living things to non-living things like people and bodies and animals and meat and mothers and fathers and queens and princes and kings and friends and former and the late and no one is ever the early and it's strange the words we use to describe things *and he's my bestest best friend mum because we know a lot about each other and . . .*

## W-s-M

on the seafront
a chap, cycling one-handed, stops
looks inside the swing bin he's carrying
tilts his head, puts his ear to the bin
as if checking the bomb's still ticking
satisfied, he continues

## Hospital Phase

Lorry delivering gas cylinders;
ambulance delivering young woman
about to be delivered of her child;
the vehicles side by side as if duetting,

the four orange flashing lights on the back of the lorry and
the four orange flashing lights on the back of the ambulance
almost but not quite in sync:
a visual representation of Reich's "Piano Phase".

## Badger Watching

*(for Steve and Charlotte)*

Watching back the footage that I shot last night,
it's the sheer relentless troughing that strikes:
a hyper badger feeding frenzy.
There's no "Excuse me sir,
could you direct me to the nearest worm bar?",
just snout-down scoffing for a full quarter-hour
then trot off done,
followed by another couple or three
doing just the same, until sated, and resetting.
It's brocktacular.

# Otters

genus *Lutra*

The word “otter” is anciently related to “water”,
and apparently signifies an aquatic creature.
Pre-eminent among all aquatic creatures,
the otter was honoured with this name.

## Ripples

and here they come now:
I sense waves with whiskers, like
otters kissing gods –

rippled, knotted zinc;
hot mocha stone and flux peaks;
globes of mirror ice;

slick fur; urchin spines;
or, if I'm pressed to decide,
grooves for swimming in –

forever afloat,
lost in a city of milk,
I shimmer outwards

## Bramble Paradox

New garden. My job's to clear the brambles,
a task that's proving worthy of Sisyphus himself.
They strangle everything from Earth to sky,
a spiky, cosmos-encircling mythomonster,
many-headed, multi-rooted.
Each time I approach, they attack me in new ways,
so I defend myself as if against the Hydra –
first gloves, then two pairs doubled;
goggles seemed the thing, as I value my sight,
till a nine-foot thornshoot smote me,
whipping my cheek and nose;
now I go into battle with a full-face visor.
This morning, they drew blood on my legs –
next, I'll be wearing chainsaw trousers.

And yet, the paradox is that of all the fruits,
blackberries are my favourite.
They are sweet in the moment and in memory:
late-summer days on the infinite common,
seeking the most night-resemblant taste bombs
to take home to gorge on
or to sieve and boil into divine seedless jam.
For something that grows on a cursèd weed,
their flavour at peak is rich, decadent even,
the juice staining lips and tongue like money and lies.

Yet these thorns grow as fast as I cut.
I fear I'll be hacking them down for the rest of time.
What's more, now they haunt my dreams and my days:
wherever I go – by the roadside, at the seaside,

in sleep's wild horrendous landscapes –
all I can see is brambles that no one will clear.

## Sea Glass

Heads down, sun on necks,
we quarter the foreshore
for accidental gems.

Here's one:
cool emerald

and another, smaller, paler.

Look, two more –
a clear thumbnail

and a
granule

of former bottle.

Later, looking back, not down:
did I find *you*, my multicolour jewel,
or did you rescue *me* from the tide?

## Code of Conduct for the Otter Club

1. The Otter Club of Great Britain is a registered enterprise pursuant to the terms of the Registered Enterprise (Mustelids) Act 2014 and otter regulations. It should not be confused with otter similarly named organisations.
2. Members must always demonstrate respect for otter members, as well as for non-otter mustelids ("affiliates").
3. Details of the club and its members may only be discussed with otters. Please respect otter members' confidentiality.
4. Please do not inconvenience or in any otter way botter otter members. An otter's first responsibility is to otter fellow otters and the reputation of the club. Otters are not rotters.
5. Please do not publicly endorse health cures or therapeutic options on behalf of the club. Otters have done so in the past, and the resultant arguments about hydrotterapy, psychotterapy, hypnotterapy and cryotterapy have caused considerable upset. Instead, otters should be united in a spirit of brotterliness and sisterliness.
6. Please desist from enquiring about when the pool heater will be fixed. The club committee is continuing its delicate negotiations with our suppliers regarding the mis-selling of a geottermal heating system that promised much but has so far delivered little, otter than occasional lukewarm bubbles.

*Errata: For "otter", please read "other" throughout, except where "otter" is clearly correct. Otterwise please contact the club for clarification.*

## Insomnambulation

There's midnight in my bones,
jet to the marrow.

Taking a night walk
to cool my jalfrezi brain,
I gaze at the fish stars in the sea sky,
the whirling shoals of silver light.

There is no scenery at all
except the schools above me:
bioluminescent lives,
the infinite wisdom of their infinite crowd.

And still the coals glow:
midnight in those bones.

## IKB

*"a Blue in itself, disengaged from all functional justification"*
*– Exhibition description of International Klein Blue, Milan, 1957*

A midnight bathroom-mirror glimpse
of two-quid baggy Primark tee
launches me to Yves Klein's world
of single-colour canvasses –

to the paint he dreamed,
suspending ultramarine
in the Rhodopas medium
to unnaturally vivid effect –

to the Tate Gallery, as was in '84;
*IKB 79*, one of Klein's huge, disengaged works
engaged with me like little else that day,
a wall of blue so blue it outblued blue itself –

to Monte Palace in Funchal,
scant decades later where
a huge framed billboard painted IKB
illuminated trees and hued the leaves –

to this, this now and here:
a two-quid baggy Primark tee
that in this harshlit setting could well be
International Klein Blue.

## a mist that appears for a little while

*(James 4:14)*

we are all transient
ephemeral as sea mist
ground frost in sun
daylilies and mayflies
top quarks and hot sparks
fleeting thoughts
synaptic lightning
snatches of song
glimpses of life
a glorious fog of swirling atoms

## Dead-Nettle Office

Pembrokeshire beach path.
I footstep past dead-nettles;
stop, now, and dive in –

purple, orchidesque
blooms like raspberry ripple
(or borscht and sour cream);

benign, hirsute leaves,
histamine-free, burn-absent
yet shape-familiar;

but the magenta
– "purple archangel", indeed –
is captivating.

I'm going nowhere;
just gonna stare into your
deep, delicate eyes.

## July's Face

July's face,
a little darker than winter's
apart from the scar above this eyebrow:
a sunken pock, lenticular pool,
still March-pallid,
time-frozen.

## Lungs and Limbs

Just for a second, the thought crossed my mind: what if all the oaks were taken from us by some disease? And it struck me like lightning. All the trees on our road, oaks, gone. The three oaks on the green, gone. The biggest tree down by the river, gone. All the oaks everywhere, gone. And the sense of loss was like losing a lung and a limb.

Just why are oaks so much to me? They are not my first memory of trees. They were not the trees in my grandparents' garden (those were silver birch). I have never lived with oaks. I don't even have a thing about acorns. And yet there they are, wisdom in wood form. And the thought of a world without them was viscerally painful, like losing a lung and a limb.

## Aurous

    beside<br>
    the River Blackwater<br>
    a dozen<br>
goldfinches<br>
    feed on<br>
golden samphire<br>
    their<br>
yellow flashes<br>
    reflecting the<br>
yellow flowers<br>
    reflecting in the water<br>
    as they ascend<br>
    melting souls

## On Newtown Lane

a magpie, startled by my approach,
VTOLs the hedgerow
and throws a blink of shadow
across the downcast snowdrops

## Wobble

vanilla

panic

otter

## Looking for Otters

No, I didn't see an otter,
not today, nor the last time, nor before.

But I did see a muntjac, curious and fearful;
sunrise, peach blush over the downs;
grebes diving, resurfacing in a different postcode;
mist 15-tog-duveting the meadow.

And I heard a laughing yaffle,
the tumbling notes of two blackcaps freestyling,
a bittern's boom, cetti's warblers erupting,
till the spectrum glow of dusk fell through the reeds.

No otters though.
Still, there's always next time.

# Ferrets and polecats

genus *Mustela*, subgenus *Putorius*

The word “ferret” comes from the Latin *furittus*,
“little thief”, referring to the animal’s legendary habit
of taking small objects and hiding them.
And now, having unearthed this nugget of etymology,
I’ll be humming Feargal Sharkey’s 1985 hit
“You Little Thief” all day.

## The Photographs

*The box I found in my great uncle's attic contained old photos, now so badly faded as to be unrecognisable, but fortunately each bore an explanatory note on the reverse in copperplate handwriting:*

"Lisbon, July 1931"

"Elsie's first steps"

"Me, engulfed in moths"

"The children, running along the Great Wall of China"

"Uncle Mike and Auntie Sally, snowbound in June"

"Pike"

"Don't know who this is or when or where"

"Alfred (2 days old)"

"Best Northern Lights ever"

"Making medlar cheese"

"Alfred with President Coolidge, shortly before the billiard table burst into flames"

"The Cenotaph, from inside"

"The garden at No. 37"

"Splitting the atom"

"Feeding the tigers"

"Melting clocks with Dalí"

"Our wedding. Shame it's so blurred."

"Elsie and me, *[illegible]* iguanas"

"Mike (after the surgery!)"

"The garden at No. 37" *[again]*

"Brussels. Or maybe Norwich."

"School sports day, St Hilda's Grammar, 1933"

"Our first Austin"

"Dearest Ivy. Rest in peace, sweet child."

"Ullapool, midnight"

"Grandad, with his ferrets"

"Grandad, with his hands heavily bandaged"

"Herding sheep with Rex and" *[photo torn, caption lost]*

"Gordon back from somewhere secret, bearing bottles of plum brandy"

"On the Shetland bus"

"Wimbledon 1922"

*[blank, apart from a heart drawn in lipstick]*

"Testing rockets with Wernher"

"The air raid shelter in Bolton Avenue"

"The End."

## Soundtrack

*(i.m. Michael Longley)*

From the bath,
morning's accompaniment

of road music from tyres of
car, car, van, car,
lorry, lorry, lorry

is cut through by dawn chorus of
blue tit, blue tit, dunnock, crow,
bullfinch, greenfinch, long-tailed tit.

## The Inglorious Deaths of the Emperors of Rome (It Is Said)

It is said that to seek fame is to seek grief.
It is said that to crave power is to crave downfall.

Of the emperors of Rome, it is said
(for none of us were there, so

we can only rely on ancient, fragmentary reports)
that many died a violent and/or inglorious death.

Caligula, we read, was stabbed by Chaerea as payback for his mockery;
Claudius was poisoned with toadstools, allegedly by his wife Agrippina;

Commodus was strangled in his bath by the athlete Narcissus;
Petronius Maximus was stoned by an angry mob and thrown into the Tiber;

Valerian, according to one account, was forced to swallow molten gold;
Caracalla was lanced while relieving himself (what a way to go);

Valentinian I died of a stroke while yelling at envoys;
Nero stabbed himself in the throat – with a little help;

Germanicus fell ill and died "under dubious circumstances";
Vespasian's end was by dysentery – a career down the toilet;

Carus was on campaign beyond the Tigris when struck by
    lightning;
Jovian, though much decorated, seems to have suffocated
    on paint fumes.

The demise of many emperors remains unknown,
their ignominy unrecorded:

perhaps some surfeited on dormice, were fed to ferrets,
or were defenestrated into a latrine.

Those who seek imperial office, beware:
your glory and power are transitory

and your downfall may be sudden.
So it is said.

## By Degrees

70 °C

My father used to twinkle when
he talked of theoretically
fashioning a teaspoon
from Wood's metal –
an alloy with a melting point of 70 degrees
and hence useless for stirring hot tea
except as a prank.

I say theoretically, but that twinkle
suggested that he might just have done it
as a young chemistry student,
just as he definitely did synthesise
a large batch of fluorescein
and smuggle it
on the Tube

to Trafalgar Square
to dye the fountains,
only to be thwarted by miscalculation
over the volume of water involved
and the amount of jossop needed
to satisfactorily render
the jets and cascades glowing.

In this day and age
such an act of intervention's
really not the done thing
(search "UK counter-terrorism legislation"),

nor are Wood's-metal-related japes
in view of the toxicity
of the cadmium and other contents.

And now I can't ask Dad whether
the spoon was a bona fide recollection
or just a potential joke from his youth:
first his memory melted
and some time later the rest of him followed,
an unfull alloy spoon
succumbing to the heat of the beverage.

## 105 °F

fever delirium
the duvet is eating me
                    meat for pillows

  I am just a pile of months
with my                                        yoghurt and
                              all these sea slugs
        yeah, feet

  I am wearing
                    wearing *all* of my clothes
          newspaper buskins and a        nice          throbe

the spoons have the power and there
                                        are so many polecats in
            this wild habitat             (brop, brop,       wheaf)
        this sack                of leaves
                         shelder        and  ennage        and

                    I am just a pile
  of
                                                       moths

## -232 °C

*(the average surface temperature of Pluto, according to NASA)*

On a deck chair,
laid out on the frozen methane hydrate – such a
bright but small sun – blue haze through the hydrocarbons –
playing bumblepuppy on the gelid beachfront –
Pluto: views of Charon, and monoxide ice cubes
in your cocktail.

## 1,000 °C

peer
through the hatch
in the oil-drum kiln

see
the glaze glow,
melt, crackle: raku

## 17 °C

At 17 degrees or above,
– RED ADMIRAL –
it doesn't matter if it's overcast:
– GREEN-VEINED WHITE, BRIMSTONE –
the transect is valid
– LARGE SKIPPER, SMALL SKIPPER –
and you can record what butterflies you see.
– PURPLE EMPEROR, HOLLY BLUE –

Now some species will fly
– PEACOCK, MARBLED WHITE –
at lower temperatures,
– SPECKLED WOOD, MEADOW BROWN –
but 17's the minimum, say the rules
– PAINTED LADY, CLOUDED YELLOW –
(14 if sunny); it's science.
– LARGE WHITE, SMALL WHITE, WALL –

At the millennium's turn
– ORANGE TIP, LARGE BLUE –
I'd regularly do counts in a local wood,
– SILVER-WASHED FRITILLARY –
and July would be the highlight;
– GATEKEEPER, RINGLET –
but now the white admirals have gone.
– WHITE ADMIRAL –

I also used to often see the erratic,
– PURPLE HAIRSTREAK –
random wingbeats of purple hairstreaks.

– PURPLE HAIRSTREAK –
Once I found one in the grass, too weak to fly;
– PURPLE HAIRSTREAK –
it climbed onto my hand, supped sweat and iridesced away.
– PURPLE HAIRSTREAK –

Four in five of our butterfly species
– SMALL TORTOISESHELL –
have fallen in numbers in the last 50 years.
– DUKE OF BURGUNDY, SMALL COPPER –
They talk to us the only way they can.
– COMMON BLUE, CHALKHILL BLUE –
Are we listening . . .
– COMMA –

## 4 °C

ice floats · · now,
while this may
not be startling
news, it is in fact
extremely odd · ·

solid forms of any
given material can
usually be relied
upon to be denser
than the liquid,

but ice being
less dense than
liquid water
makes $H_2O$
anomalous · ·

at four degrees C,
water's at its densest,
the molecules packed
tight thanks to a
balance of forces:

the kinetic energy
keeping the molecules
moving apart and the
bonds pulling them
together match · ·

both above and
below this point,
water expands
and becomes
less dense · ·

the previously
temporary hydrogen
bonds of the
fluid become
permanent · ·

the molecules
take up a more
open, hexagonal
lattice structure
as water freezes · ·

the outcome of
this particular
intermolecular
tango is that if
the temperature

of water on the
surface of a body
falls below four, it
stays on that surface
rather than sinking · ·

and if it then
freezes, the ice
becomes a layer
of insulation,
protecting life below · ·

but my head swims
with polar molecules,
covalent bonds
and clustering
electrons · ·

so if you ask me why
ice floats, I'll skip
attempts at explanation
and just respond:
because it *must*

## 0 K (ABSOLUTE ZERO)

*"The producing of Cold is a thing very worthy the Inquiſition, both for uſe and diſcloſure of cauſes. For Heat and Cold are Natures two hands, whereby ſhe chiefly worketh; and Heat we have in readineß, in reſpect of the Fire: But for Cold, we muſt ſtay till it cometh, or ſeek it in deep Caves, or high Mountains; and when all is done, we cannot obtain it in any great degree: For Furnaces of Fire are far hotter than a Summers Sun, but Vaults or Hills are not much colder than a Winters Froſt." – Francis Bacon,* Sylva Sylvarum: or, A Naturall Historie in Ten Centuries *(1627)*

Absolute zero: the mouth of a cave in which there is not merely emptiness but absence – absence of heat, and, in particular, absence of particular motion. To approach this zero, one must get the temperature down by any means absolutely necessary – but is cold necessarily "down"? We may visualise a thermometer falling, going down to zero mathematically, but is it not the case that the colder the temperature one reaches, the harder it is to get colder? Hence, the difficulty rises as the coldness increases. (And yet it is true that we refer to the temperature "falling".) Absolute zero itself is unattainable, at time of writing, and possibly at any time short of infinity, as attaining it would require an infinite amount of work. Nevertheless, ingenuity has resulted in conjuring temperatures of merely a few billionths of a degree above 0 K; 38 picokelvin was reached by "interaction-driven quadrupole-mode excitation of a Bose–Einstein condensate with a magnetic lens" – a deep cave of science, whose meaning and significance are largely frozen: an arctic vault of thermodynamic absolution buried on a distant, icy moon.

*"There is an opinion, that the Moon is Magnetical of Heat, as the Sun is of Cold and Moiſture." – Bacon, ibid.*

# Wolverines

genus *Gulo*

The French for wolverine is *glouton,* i.e. “glutton”,
due to the animal’s reputation
for being a ravenous predator.
The Latin name *Gulo gulo* means “glutton glutton”,
and the Old World subspecies is *Gulo gulo gulo,*
which is perhaps putting it a bit strong.

## Stage

traffic shot the floodpool
into the twiggy hedgerow –

now a dream city
of icy towers awaits
tales to be set among
its backlit sci-fi spires

## *Ugagn*

*(basert på et intervju med en reindriftssame)*

*Naturen e vårres plass å leve i.*
*Men jerven gjør så mye ugagn.*

*Æ driver jo med rein. Vi e liksom*
*oppvekst med rovdyr. Jerver dræp jo rein,*
*men det gjør gaupe og bjørn og ørn også.*

*Samer har alltid hadd en veldig respekt for bjørn –*
*bjørn har jo en veldig sterk urkraft –*
*og samme har man hadd for gaupe, men jerven . . .*

*Gaupe kommer inn og så dræp ho på en fin måte,*
*og ho sprer ikke rein,*
*og jager ikke rein på den måten som jerven gjør.*

*Jerven e så seig; det e bare hel muskel hele jerven.*
*Han springer ikke så veldig fort,*
*men han kan holde en jevn tempo i mange mil når han fær.*

*Han jager og sprer rein veldig mye.*
*Visse tider så dræp han bare og græv det ned til seinere.*
*Seinast i går fant æ en rein som jerven hadde dræpt.*

*Æ veit ikke nån samer som respekterer jerven,*
*for han gjør så mye problem for oss.*
*Så mye ugagn.*

*Derfor e det veldig mange som si jerver,*
*de e Satans verk.*

## Havoc

*(based on my interview with a Sámi reindeer herder)*

Nature is our place to live in.
But wolverines cause so much havoc.

I'm a reindeer herder. We kind of
grow up with predators. Wolverines kill reindeer,
but so do lynx and bears and eagles.

The Sámi have always had a great respect for bears –
bears have a very powerful primitive force –
and we feel the same about lynx, but wolverines . . .

Lynx are quite refined, the way they kill,
and they don't scatter the reindeer,
and they don't chase them the way wolverines do.

Wolverines are tough; they're like solid muscle.
They can't run so fast,
but they can keep up a steady pace for mile after mile.

They chase and scatter the reindeer a lot.
Sometimes they just kill and bury it for later.
Last night, I found a reindeer that a wolverine had killed.

I don't know any Sámi who respect wolverines,
because they cause so many problems for us.
So much havoc.

That's why many say that wolverines
are the Devil's work.

## The Crossing

The zebra crossing on Wyke Road
has four white stripes,
one for each leg of the beast.
The reflective paint that forms them is
unevenly applied,
impasto on tarmac,
as if trampled by the herd.

The beacon on the southern side
is held up by a bracket,
architecturally cobwebbed.
The spiders' flyless threads have caught
a single dandelion seed;
freed from the clock,
another trap was waiting.

## Spread Thinly

So much to do, trying to look after everyone,
you have to spread yourself more thinly.
“If I spread myself thinly enough,” you think,
“maybe I can reach a bit further,
maybe I can be in more than one place at a time.
As long as they’re not too far apart.”

So, sometimes you put yourself through a mangle
to make yourself thinner, more elastic.
Through the mangle. Over and over again.
And with each pass through, you can spread out more.
All so you can do everything, be everything to everyone.
But you’re thinner. Less you.

There comes a point where the bones have long gone,
shattered by the metal rollers,
and you’re just stretched flesh and skin.
And as you spread out more, you’re that little less effective,
because there’s that little less of you.
But you have to keep on,
because whatever you do, it’s not enough,
so you keep stretching more and more.

Gradually, you start to lose opacity, pass into translucence.
Other things, visible right through you.
You become invisible, but you’re still trying to
be everywhere at once, do everything for everyone.
Any notion of your self has long since gone.
And you’re still stretching your fabric, down to a single
atom thin,

until all the bonds break down, and you no longer exist. And then you do it all again the next day.

## *Le Mot injuste*

just the fatigue
when talking, can't find the words
must've fallen off the mental shelf

often the wrong worms come out
given up on pronouns
sometimes can't finish sentences
the thoughts dissolve before even

now taken to using placeholders
need to [verb] the [noun]
and hope others manage to grok the parsnip
not parsnip, the other thing

## Aral

*"Clearly one of the worst . . . environmental disasters of the world."*
*– Ban Ki-moon, former UN Secretary-General*

*The Aral Sea, once the world's third-largest lake, has shrunk to one-tenth of its original size, due to decades of ruinous mismanagement of the rivers that historically fed it. The disappearing waters have left in their wake a poisonous desert, ecosystem collapse, loss of livelihoods, chronic health problems and all the other hallmarks of large-scale human meddling.*

we have been
shrunk our former
conscio usness now
fragmentary been bled
of life toxic salty our lungs
once dust full dust
toxic salty dust and vi dust
tal toxic salty dust now toxic
gasp fitful toxic salty dust toxic salty
ly we toxic salty dust toxic salty dust toxic salty
float dust toxic salty dust toxic salty dust
sink toxic salty dust toxic salty dust toxic salty dust
de toxic salty dust toxic salty dust toxic salty dust to xic
sicc toxic salty dust toxic salty dust toxic salty dust toxic salty
ate in dust toxic salty dust toxic salty dust toxic salty dust toxic
to the toxic sal ty dust toxic salty dust toxic salty dust tox ic
relief salty dust toxic salty dust toxic salty dust toxic salty dust
of obliv toxic salty dust toxic salty dust toxic salty dust dust dust
ion we toxic salty dust toxic salty dust toxic salty dust toxic
have salty dust toxic salty dust toxic salty dust to xic
been salty dust toxic salty dust toxic salty dust toxi c
salty dust toxic salty dust toxic salty dust toxic sal ty
dust toxic salty dust toxic salty dust toxic salty d us t
toxic salty dust toxic salty dust toxic salty dust
toxic salty dust toxic salty dust toxic salty d us t
toxic salty dust toxic dust toxic salty dust tox ic
salty dust toxic salty dust toxic s a l ty du s t
to xic salty dust toxic s a l ty
salt y
toxic
dust

## Elusive

One day
I will write the perfect poplar poem,
eulogise their dazzling metal leaves
caught in low-slung, wistful autumn sun.

Likewise,
my soul aspires to capture oystercatchers'
nature, essence, oystercatcher-ness,
through the means of words alone, at last.

And yet
the most elusive subject yet is you –
you who simply cannot be defined,
save by "love" and similar graspless terms.

Till then
I will keep on trying, please forgive:
poplar verses, oystercatcher haiku,
sonnets, couplets, quatrains for my love.

## Supermarket Sketches

I.

"Sorry," I say, the nose of my trolley
   having grazed the side of hers.
"Sorry," she counters, as if she had
   any reason to proffer regret.
It's like the hollow metallic clank of collision
   triggers an apology reflex in us
or chimes the first note of some primeval tune
   summoning us to dance an excuse-me.

II.

"It's a thing of beauty, that,"
she remarks to a colleague,
standing back to survey the results
of her shampoo-shelf tidying,
revelling in the simple pleasure
of enforcing elegance
on the mundane.

III.

Lady leaving
Morrisons
cradling loaf like
newborn child – –

IV.

Slightly in the way, I move my trolley,
allowing a staff member to unpack
Tropicana juice onto the shelf

and somewhere in a misfired memory
Wham! starts playing – –
a drink is poured into a pool.

V.

Waitrose car park, 8 p.m., February:
trees spotlit in the blackness
and robins' song echoing.

Sure, they may in fact be
aggressively marking out territory
but it sounds like – feels like – unbound joy.

VI.

Elderly gent's
shopping trolley:
sixteen pots of cappuccino mousse
and some soup.

VII.

Leaving the shop with my milk, juice,
impulse-buy chocolate fudge ice cream
and other miscellaneous edibles.
Ahead of the trolley,
a shimmer-green damselfly dances,
brings me back to the *real* real world.

VIII.

Took the long way to the shop,
over the ford bridge, then stopped –
low evening sun through newborn leaves
on the trees that overhang the river.
Birdsong, water running, far traffic,
and fifty years ago a tractor taking Chantry Ford,
following the river fifty yards to the fields
where the supermarket now stands.

# Martens

genus *Martes*

The Romanian word for marten is *jder*.
I can give no reason for mentioning that here,
other than the word's (to me) pleasingly odd appearance.

## The Eyes of a Pine Marten

looking into the eyes of a pine marten
there was no holding of gaze
there was no recognition of shared experience
there was no deep time
there was me looking at you looking at me

there was an instant and then moving on
there was no evident fear
but no inclination to remain
there was a life lived at a different pace to mine
there was metabolic urgency

sure, I'd longed for that moment for decades
and I will recall you for many of your lifetimes
but you had no reason to remember me
and your interest was fleeting
in a being that could be nothing but a threat

## The Thief of Time

All year, every year,
I look out at the street light opposite
that sprouts up through the middle of a tree.
At night, the light illuminates the leaves,
leaves patterned shadows on the road.

Every year at this time
the leaves turn red, and drop, but not
before they're transformed electrically
into shimmering copper explosions.
After that, it's just another street light.

And every year
I fully intend to write a perfect poem on
the simple beauty of this juxtaposition,
two things put too close together,
but resulting in unintended beauty.

And every year
I don't – I can't – get round to it.
Or I try and fail, and fail again.
Somehow I can't make it into a poem.
And this doesn't count, it's not the one.

So every year
I'm left with another year's regret.
I measure my life, count my years
in procrastinated unwritten poems
about that street light and that tree.

## Triolet on Watching a Video of a Sable Playing in a Bucket of Snow

The sable dives into the snow
and frolics with unbounded glee.
It corkscrews down – just watch it go! –
the sable dives into the snow;
of joy, it knows more than we know
who gaze at shimmering TV.
The sable dives into the snow
and frolics with unbounded glee.

## Precipitation

The very sky is crying for you.
The tears are running
down the cheeks of all the houses, all the trees,
bouncing off the cars and roads,
streaming into the rivers,
heading to the seas,
to rise again to sorry cumulonimbus,
ready for another day's tragedy.

## Choose Your Exit

*(for Crysse)*

If compelled to choose my exit,
my selection's this:
teleport me off to Venus,
for preference Beta Regio.

Should I really have to leave here,
let me join Venera 9,
beneath the amber acid skies
on loveless basalt slopes.

Yes, I'll be choked and boiled
and crushed and dissolved,
but to see that scene so familiarly other,
have one Earth second on the second Earth . . .

And if I have to wait until
the tech required is ripe –
interplanetary teleportation –
so be it. There's no rush.

## Three Pebbles

two dragonflies –
the crackle and fizz
as their wings clash

*

a score of crows
shine briefly white in flight –
perfect angle of sun

*

red admiral
glides across the brook –
peace returns

## *In memoriam* the CERN Stone Marten

Curiosity can lead us down strange alleys.
We reveal new, odd knowledge every day,
limits, horizons, perspectives.
It's why the Large Hadron Collider was built –
to discover something already believed to exist:
the Higgs boson, popularly referred to as
the "God particle".

Curiosity can lead us down dangerous alleys.
What was the stone marten looking for
that day in twenty sixteen
when it entered the transformer at CERN?
Evidence for dark matter? God? Food?
High-voltage cables are short on nutrition, but long on
electrocution.
Dining on wiring, it found the ultimate answer to all
questions of existence.

## Short Circuit

earthbound,
deskbound at an upstairs window
facing a queue of bronchial oaks
(moss-green highlights
on dark, stark branches)

and the squirrels,
arcing from outstretched branch
to opposing outstretched branch,
short-circuiting, proving
you don't need wings to fly

## Cake

Last night she dreamt she was a Battenburg cake.
Woke me, complaining I'd stolen all the marzipan duvet.

# Epilogue

*Writing about mustelids is somewhat problematic. Yes, they are (mostly) cute animals, but they are (mostly) cute animals that kill.*

*They are voracious predators – sometimes of things we like or care about: baby hares, Orkney voles; sometimes of things we might view negatively: grey squirrels, invasive foreign crayfish; sometimes of things that represent our livelihood: fish, chickens, reindeer.*

*All European mustelids have been persecuted; in some cases culled; in some cases almost eradicated; in some cases they are recovering.*

*Was there a natural balance and humans have just messed it all up? It wouldn't be the first time.*

## Building the Perfect Mustelid

Fascinating beasts, mustelids.
And each has its own USP:
for badgers, it's their distinctive stripes;
pine martens can partially retract their claws;
otters have sweet-scented spraint (and are amphibious);
ermines have an air of nobility;
weasels are the villains of literature;
ferrets recall trousers and 70s sitcoms;
and a wolverine can take down an elk.

Could one combine the best of each
and build the perfect mustelid –
a greatest-hits highlights package,
a must-have of mustelidae?
Entranced by this reverie, I searched
for ideas, references, inspiration –
previous attempts to assemble such a best-of,
albeit in imaginary or stuffed form.
My mining online turned up:

a stuffed badger that had been made into a theremin;

a cream *Martes* with added wings and antlers,
tagged "Real taxidermy full mount chimera sable";

numerous desiccated antique otters
looking distinctly angry and bitey,
unlike the frolicsome, cute water babies
depicted on the socials;

the ratipede (a dozen dead rats
expertly and horrifically transformed
into one many-legged nightmare-trigger –
but rats aren't mustelids, so it doesn't count);

vintage ermines in various stages of distress and moult;

taxidermy weasel slap bracelets;

a very snarly stuffed and mounted wolverine,
only four thousand dollars.

Every single example
diminished and mocked the original,
trivialising the creature into a grotesque outrage,
for that is what humans do.

So much for building the perfect mustelid.

This thought experiment brings itself
to its inevitable conclusion:
leave them as they are –
perfection cannot be improved.

# Acknowledgements

*Some of these poems first appeared in the following journals, to whom I express my thanks:*

And Other Poems: *The Man in the Moon Sends a Voice Note*
Flights: *Grey and Yellow (which also appeared in the anthology* Take Flight 2023*), Hospital Phase, Parabola, Time's Meadow*
The Hooghly Review: *70 °C*
Macrame Literary Journal: *Stoating*
MoonLit Getaway: *The Eyes of a Pine Marten, Supermarket Sketches I (as Supermarket Sketch: Tune)*

*I am deeply grateful to Per Thomas for taking the time to talk to me about wolverines.* Giitu *– thank you – for allowing me to tell your story. My thanks also go to Hildegunn Breivik and Eli Synnøve Breivik Forthun for arranging the interview with Per, and to Reidar Djupvik for his invaluable and iterative assistance on many points with the Norwegian text.*

*Profuse thanks to Karen Brazier for sharing the encounter that inspired Stoating.*

*I wish to thank the members of Trowbridge Stanza for input and suggestions on certain poems.*

*Delicious thanks to Ecco Gelato of Dorset for inspiring the cover painting.*

*Love and thanks, as always, to Steph for her patience and encouragement.*

# Index

This is Leon.
Leon is not a fan of otters,
for reasons he hopes are obvious.
He thinks badgers are stylish, though.

Printed and bound by CPI Group (UK) Ltd, Croydon, CR0 4YY
01/08/2025
01929133-0001